A GLIMPSE OF KOOTENAY LAKE HOSPITAL: HISTORY

We go back to the year 1893. On the grounds of the old hospital a 10-12 bed frame building was constructed. The hospital operated growing from a little house to a bigger house, altered, adapted, rebuilt in 1916-18. Finally deserted in December 1958 when the Society's operation moved to the present location on View Street and the name was changed from General Hospital to District Hospital.

Hospital charter was April 1, 1893. 1899 the hospital was mainly for miners, no maternity at that time. Maternity patients were looked after in private homes. 1899 the "FIRST AID TO NELSON HOSPITAL" was loosely organized. Called "THE LADIES HOSPITAL AID SOCIETY". Later in October 9, 1931, "THE KOOTENAY LAKE GENERAL HOSPITAL AUXILIARY immerged. There were 40 Charter Members. Name was changed in 1958 to "KOOTENAY LAKE DISTRICT HOSPITAL".

Early meetings were held in the Nurses Residence, later in private homes. From there it was moved to the Board Room where it is presently being held, the second Friday of each month at 2 p.m.

Early Auxiliary members (these were the depression years) did a variety of interesting things, gathered fruit and vegetables from Community. They preserved it and donated it to the HOSPITAL KITCHENS. They got into the sewing end of the needs. They made pajamas, gowns, curtains and diapers and they even purchased the CUTLERY for the patients.

They provided Christmas gifts for the patients who found themselves in the hospital over the holiday. They made the tray favors for special occasions. Today this is being done by the Candy Strippers. At that time they launched a service that continues to the present day that is providing materials. Finger puppets are also provided for the Lab and Emergency Department for the young patients who are disturbed by the procedures they may have to go through. They have a Gift Shop that provides many things for sale. Including knitting, stuffed toys and many other items. They also provided emergency pack consisting of a tooth brush and paste for patients.

Fund raising has ranged from bridge parties, teas, dances, raffles, tag days, catering, rummage-garage-bake-book and auction sales, wine and cheese parties, canteen cart, sale of knitted baby goods and chemotherapy caps and ostomy bags, to T.V. rentals, concession stand and gift shop.

In 1931, funds raised were $836.00 to over $6,000 in 1990. 1998 is approx. $13,000. These funds have helped to purchase articles from the mundane, such as linoleum, bedpans, coffee urns, chairs, drapes, and mattresses to the more exotic sounding such as resuscitators, gastroscopes, laparoscopes, spectrophotometers, bronchoscopes, tracheal intubation fiberscopes, portable isolets, patient lifts, pulse rate monitor, cardiac monitor fan out, cardiac arrest "crash carts", I.V. infusion pumps, commode chairs, wheel chairs, patient operated beds, exercise bicycle for physiotherapy, as well as completely furnishing two patient non smoking lounges.

In 1961 the Lord's Prayer that was spoken in unison was replaced by the Auxilian Prayer.

Hospital tours are conducted of the hospital, whenever there is a request, usually it is the school children.

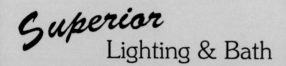
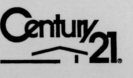

NOTICE TO THE READER

In this book, the authors, editors, medical and technical advisors, or publisher have done their best to describe each affliction or condition in a language that children can understand and at the same time describing the situation in simple terms. The book has been written so that after a qualified person has made the diagnosis it can be read to the child to relieve some of the anxieties that often cause children to be afraid.

Revised Edition 1996
ISBN 1-55056-596-6 PROGRAMS
Children's Programs
Jewett, Texas/Wpg. MB
1-800-447-8374

Authors: A. (Tony) Rhodes-Marriott, Oliver G. Deets & Bob Allowski
Editors: Charlene Natyna, John Lwiwski, Kelly Erickson,
Title: Diane Henderson
Interior Illustrations: Rita Albert
Cover Photography: Joe Knysh Photo Services
Cover: Kelly Robinson, Andrea Erickson & Steve Childerhouse
Printed and bound in Canada
Published by Friesens Printing

A Message to all Parents

As your child grows, their quest for knowledge increases immensely from the time they learn to walk and talk. Your children will eventually ask you why they get a fever, a cough, a headache; what happens when they go for x-rays, a check-up or to have a broken bone fixed. This book works on the principle that knowledgeable, informed children and parents are the best combination to reducing fears.

It is with great pleasure that we bring to you and your family "SICK BUT NOT SCARED", a book that contains brief and concise "overviews" of what your child could expect with each affliction or illness. The book is intended for children under the age of 9 and is written in words, language and illustrations that they can understand. The book is written in alphabetical order to make it easier to find each topic listed in the front table of contents.

Parents can help immensely with removing children's fears and concerns throughout their lives by not giving them 'food for thought' prior to going for a doctor or dentist appointment or a hospital stay. Children listen (and remember later) with great interest when you talk about how painful it was for Aunt Debbie when she had to have a tooth removed or about Uncle Dan's allergic reaction to a certain medicine. Months and years down the road, if and when they ever contact the disease or illness, their fear of it can be much more harmful to them than the actual treatment.

The intent of the writers of this book was for both parent and child to read through the areas together to gain an insight to many conditions that a child or their friends or family may face during their early years.

INTRODUCING .. OLLIE THE OWL

Hi Kids!!! My name is Ollie the Wise Ole Owl and you'll see me many times in this book with lots of wise health tips for you and your family.

Tips like why flossing your teeth is so important, how to keep your body strong and healthy as well as safe.

I will also answer many questions that children have like "How does my heart work?" "Why do I breathe?" "Where does the burger and fries go that I eat for dinner?"

Whenever you see me in the book, you will find a special message from me to you.

Table of Contents

General

Ollie The Owl

WHO IS A DOCTOR?

A Doctor is the name for a lady or a man who knows a lot about the human body and who knows how to treat it. After they have finished grade 12, these people would carry on to a special school for the next 4 - 7 years, learning all about how the human body works and what to do when certain illness and disease occur within a person's body.

A VISIT TO THE DOCTOR'S OFFICE

During the months and years to come, it is important for you to have regular check-ups with the doctor and dentist to ensure that you are growing into a strong and healthy boy or girl. There are a number of regular tests that the doctor may do in order to find out if all of your body systems are OK.

When you arrive at the doctor's office for your first checkup, your mom or dad will be asked by a nurse or receptionist a great many questions to learn every detail of your health background. The doctor will want to know about your family medical history as it often relates to your personal health as you are growing.

Because the doctor is usually a busy person, you may have to wait in a "waiting room" for a few minutes, which is an area where you can look at books or play with a few toys. This is an area where children should not be too loud as it would disturb other waiting patients. When the doctor is ready to see you, the receptionist or a nurse will ask your mom or dad to bring you to a treatment room. Usually the doctor will not be in the room when you get there but will join you shortly.

When you go to the doctor's office, quite often it is only for a check-up to see if all your body functions are working properly. On the following pages, you will find some of the more common tests that the doctor might do. You can be very helpful to your doctor during the examination if you will keep as relaxed as possible.

CHECK YOUR TEMPERATURE -

Everyone's natural body temperature is 98.6 Fahrenheit / 37.0 Celsius. The doctor will place a small glass tube called a thermometer in your mouth, or will place an instrument in your ear to take your temperature. This only takes a couple of minutes and doesn't hurt at all. This is to make sure that your body has the right amount of heat inside.

X - RAY'S - This is when the doctor needs to look at the bones inside your body but of course he can't see them through your skin. An X-ray machine is a camera that can look through your skin and take a picture of your insides. Like a real camera that takes pictures, you don't feel a thing when you have an X-ray.

CHEST X RAY

CHECKING YOUR EARS - The doctor may check inside your ears to make sure that they are OK. He will use a small instrument with a light at the end of it that will help the doctor see inside your ears. The instrument is usually cold so that is the only thing that you may feel.

TAKING YOUR BLOOD PRESSURE - Inside each of your bodies, blood flows which gives you life. Just as your body has a normal temperature, there is a certain pressure your blood should be at inside to be healthy. The doctor or nurse will place a piece of cloth around your upper arm and will pump it up with air. They will let the air out slowly (takes about 20 seconds), and by doing so, it will let them know what your blood pressure is.

CHECKING YOUR HEART AND LUNGS - The doctor may use a stethoscope, to check to see if your heart and lungs are OK. A stethoscope is a small shiny metal object with tubes at the end of it. The doctor puts one end of the stethoscope in their ears and the other end is placed on your chest or back. They will move the stethoscope around several times and may ask you to take deep breaths which will help them hear better. The stethoscope is usually cold so this is all you will feel.

CHECKING YOUR REFLEXES -

The doctor will usually have you sit on the edge of a table and will take a small soft rubber hammer and tap you just below your knees. This is to check to see if your body reflexes are working properly. This doesn't hurt, it just feels funny.

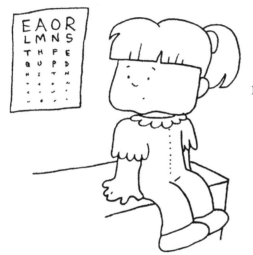

CHECKING YOUR EYES - The

doctor will take a small pen size light and shine it in your eyes to see if they work properly. The doctor might also ask you to look at a chart of all different size letters, numbers or lines. You will have to stand or sit far away from the chart and tell the doctor which letters, numbers and lines that you can see and which ones you can't.

CHECKING YOUR THROAT-

The doctor will ask you to open your mouth and he will put a tongue depressor (looks like a popsicle stick) on your tongue to hold it down so he can look inside. He will be checking your glands inside your mouth to see if everything is OK and may wipe the inside of your throat with a cotton swab.

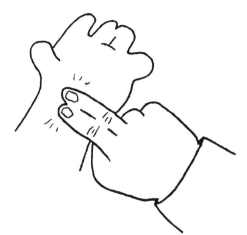

CHECKING YOUR PULSE - This
means finding out how fast your heart is
beating. The doctor or nurse will place their
finger on your wrist to feel your pulse and will
write this number down on your chart (the
doctor's record of you). When you are younger,
your heart beats faster to make sure your body
has a good supply of blood which carries food
while you are growing.

CHECKING YOUR WEIGHT &

HEIGHT - The nurse or receptionist will also
check to see how tall you are and how much weight
you've gained since your last check up. This is
important for the doctor to know to ensure that you are
growing up healthy and strong.

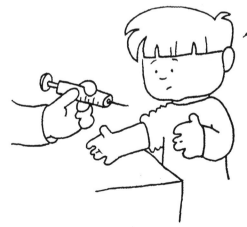

TAKING A BLOOD SAMPLE -
The doctor can find out a lot of information
about your body by taking a small amount of
blood out by a needle. The needle is a small
plastic tube with a pin on the end and feels
like a mosquito bite when the nurse puts it
into your arm. You are not to move your arm
when this is done and the little sting will go
away in a few minutes.

TAKING A URINE SAMPLE - Just like the blood sample the doctor can find out some things about your body from your urine. The doctor or nurse might ask you to go into the washroom to pee into a special container. The nurse will then take the container of pee to have it checked.

***** A MESSAGE TO ALL *****

ABOUT DRUGS - From a very early age kids hear the word "drugs", usually in the negative form. However, the authors of this book felt it important to point out that there are **GOOD** drugs and then there are **BAD** drugs. Good drugs are medicines in that a doctor tells you to take to help make you feel healthier, stronger and to relieve pain and can be bought at a pharmacy or a drug store. Bad drugs are not given out by doctors, physicians or drug stores and they can seriously damage your body. In order to lead the best possible life, children should only take medicines when they are required and **ALWAYS ALWAYS SAY "NO" TO BAD DRUGS!!**

THE WAITING ROOM COUNTING GAME
"For parents & children to do together"

The time spent in a waiting room may be an anxious time for a child. Their fear of the unknown is often worse than any treatment could be. Simply have the child face away from you and using your finger.... draw on the child's back random numbers and letters. While they are busy guessing what you have drawn, it will quickly take the child's mind off anxious moments & may cause a few laughs too if they are ticklish. Progress onto simple words such as cat, dog, etc., if the child is of appropriate age.

ABRASIONS - When you scrape a part of your body, such as your hand, elbows, or knees, the part that gets all bloody and sore is called an abrasion. That's where the skin is scratched off and the blood beneath the skin oozes through. Sometimes it can hurt a bit, but not for very long. To heal an abrasion, you should first wash the area and pick out any pieces of dirt that are stuck in there. To prevent infection, the wound should be cleaned very well and covered with a bandage, or a special piece of sterile gauze, called "dressing."

ADENOIDS - Trouble with your adenoids will give you problems breathing and it may seem like you have a cold all the time. What happens is that some parts of your breathing passages swell up and are almost blocked off. The doctor will usually give you some medication. If it keeps happening over and over again, you may have to go into the hospital to get them fixed.

BED WETTING -At one time or another this may have happened to you. During the night while you are sleeping, your muscle which holds the urine inside your body relaxes and lets it all run out. This is nothing to be alarmed or embarrassed about and there are a number of reasons why this happens such as infections, allergies or just being in a very deep sleep. It is really not necessary to receive treatment until school age at which time a doctor might suggest some medications or monitoring systems (where a special alarm wakes you when you start to wet your pj's.)

ACNE - In your skin, there are thousands of tiny openings called pores that allow your skin to breathe. When these pores get plugged (up) with dirt and oil, they get (all) red and inflamed and pimples form. When someone has many pimples, perhaps on their face, their back, or their chest, we say they have acne. Many people get acne when they become a teenager. That's when our bodies start changing from a kid's to an adult's body (this period is called 'puberty'). For normal acne, a dermatologist (a doctor for your skin) will prescribe a lotion to put on the acne to help clear it up in a few weeks.

A. I. D. S - A.I.D.S. is the short name for Acquired Immune Deficiency Syndrome. Your immune system is what fights off disease and keeps your body healthy. With AIDS, the immune system is no longer working as it should and the body cannot protect itself against infections.

OLLIE - WHAT ARE BIRTHMARKS?

Well basically, birthmarks are marks on your skin that you are born with. Some people have birthmarks that are small and some have larger ones. They can come in many different colors & shapes and sizes and can be found on various parts of the body. Birthmarks are common. While some may look unusual, they are harmless and nothing to worry about.

ALLERGIES - Sometimes a person's body will decide that it doesn't want to accept a certain food that has been eaten, or something that is in its environment. This is called an allergic reaction. For example peanuts, dust, animals, dairy products, and pollen from flowers, are some of the things which people have allergic reactions to. There are many different kinds of allergic reactions. Some of

13

the most common reactions are: eyes getting puffy; swelling of the throat; sneezing; and sometimes the skin develops a rash. A doctor will test for allergies by placing tiny amounts of different substances on your skin to see how it reacts, or do a blood test. There are many medicines to help your body fight allergies, or you may just have to try to avoid whatever it is that causes your body to have an allergic reaction.

ALZHEIMER'S - We know what your thinking.... Kids & Alzheimer's??? Alzheimer's is a condition that affects older folks (possibly a grandparent or elderly neighbor) where there is a gradual memory loss of recent events and ability to learn new stuff. We all forget things from time to time however with Alzheimer's it gets harder and harder to remember. People with Alzheimer's will misplace objects, become confused, anxious and restless. We should all try to understand that the loss of memory is not their fault.

OLLIE.....WHAT'S A BLADDER AND WHAT DOES IT DO?

A bladder is inside your body and collects all of the waste fluids your body produces. After enough fluids builds up in your bladder, it will tell your brain that it is time to go and empty it and that's when you have to go to the bathroom. This is something that will happen to you a number of times a day and is part of life.

ANEMIA

ANEMIA - Everybody needs a certain amount of iron in their blood. Anemia occurs when you do not have enough

iron, either because you are not eating enough of the proper foods - like meat, or broccoli - that have lots of iron in them, or because your body is having trouble absorbing iron. You may feel tired all the time, or have rapid breathing and pulse, and pale, or yellowish skin. Anemia can be corrected by eating more foods that are high in iron, or by taking iron pills (or vitamins with iron).

ANOREXIA NERVOSA - When some children (usually older children) stop eating for long periods of time they may have an eating disorder called Anorexia Nervosa. This really means a nervous loss of appetite (not hungry) and most often happens to females. Thinking they are too fat - they starve themselves to lose weight. This is something no one should do as it destroys healthy body tissue and can make you very sick. Working with a special doctor who knows a lot about this disorder will help a person with Anorexia Nervosa.

HEY KIDS - Did you know that there are over 100,000 miles of Blood Vessels in the grown human body. Most of them are so microscopic (very very tiny) that the human eye can not see them. Blood vessels carry life giving food to every cell in your body.

APPENDICITIS - Your appendix is a tube-like piece of skin inside your body just to the right of your belly button and is about the size of your little finger. Sometimes the appendix gets infected and has to be taken out. This is done with surgery where you would have to stay at the hospital for a couple of days. It is a very simple operation which takes only a couple of hours to complete and you'll be feeling as good as new in just a few short weeks. A small scar will be the only evidence left (an inch or two long) that you had the surgery.

ARTHRITIS - Arthritis is the condition when your joints in your body (fingers, toes, ankles, knees, elbows) swell up. Your joints will become puffy, swollen and red and may be a bit sore. There are a number of treatments that can be done depending on the type of arthritis that you have .

ASTHMA - Your lungs are like two big balloons that air comes into and goes out of. Asthma is a common condition of the lungs when it becomes harder and harder to breath and get the oxygen into our bodies and blood streams. The tubes that the air

goes through get narrower and makes it harder for you to breathe. You may have to use an **inhaler** or take other medications.

OLLIE.....WHAT ARE BONES?

Believe it or not, there are 206 bones in the fully grown body. Bones are very important along with muscles, tendons, and other body tissues which we need to be able to walk, run and play. Bones are also the key area where blood is made in the body. Sometimes, when enough pressure is placed against one of the bones in your body, it will break and hurt quite a lot. Don't worry because bones can heal themselves if they are placed in a cast (which keeps the broken bones from moving). It takes several weeks for a broken bone to heal and the length of time to heal depends on which bone you break.

BITES - A bite is when an insect or an animal either breaks through or grabs your skin with their stinger or teeth. At the very least, these bites are unpleasant and can hurt a lot depending on what bites you. If it is an insect that bites you, scratching may lead to an infection. The best thing to do is ask a grown-up to put ice on it to relieve the sting and itching, and to use other lotions or remedies.

Most animal bites are by cats, dogs, squirrels and other small critters. Immediate medical attention should be given and have the bite checked out at the doctor's office or hospital may be necessary.

BLISTERS - These are caused by something that is too tight or too hard, rubbing on your skin. They will often be like little balloons filled with water. If they burst, take the old skin off, put some cream on (the area may be tender) & cover with a clean bandaid.

OLLIE..... WHEN I'M PLAYING WITH MY FRIENDS IN THE PLAYGROUND AND RUNNING AROUND MY HOUSE, I HAVE TO STOP BECAUSE I RUN OUT OF BREATH. WHY?

Breathing is something every human being in the world has to do and is automatic. You don't even have to think about it to do it. Sometimes during sports or other physical activities, your breathing gets faster because your body needs more air (oxygen) to work. After you stop and rest for a few minutes from whatever you were doing, then your breathing will slow down to it's normal level. If you play a certain sport - let's say soccer, the more you practice and play the game, each time breathing will be a little easier.

BLOOD POISONING - There is blood inside of your body that circulates through your veins bringing nutrients to all of the body cells.

Blood poisoning is when something bad gets into your blood stream and makes it sick. You can get it many ways, sometimes from stepping on a rusty nail or some other object. You may see red streaks on your skin and will have to go see the doctor to have him or her help you get better.

BRONCHITIS - This is like a really bad cold and cough that does not want to get better. Because all the bad cold stuff gets inside your chest and fills it up, you may have trouble

breathing or sleeping. The doctor will give you medicine to make you feel better.

OLLIE..... WHAT ARE BRACES AND WHY DO I NEED THEM?

BRACES - There are braces for your teeth and braces for your legs or arms. In both cases, braces are a combination of plastic and metal that help make our teeth, arms and legs straighter. For teeth, braces can be placed on your teeth for up to a couple of years with regular visits to the doctor to have them adjusted. Braces on legs or arms, help give them extra support.

BRUISES - Ouch!! Yes, bruises can be ouchees. When an area of your body gets hit, a blood vessel may break and a bruise may form. The bruise will change the color of your skin to yellow, blue, green or purple. It will be sore and will take a little while to go away.

BURNS - When something very very hot touches a part of your body and injures the skin, we call this a burn. Depending on how severe the burn is, you may experience pain, swelling of the area, blisters and your skin may turn a reddish color. Sometimes the injured skin may peel away as your body is repairing itself by growing a layer of new skin. The burn may have to be placed in cool water or have a sterile bandage put on.

OLLIE.... BESIDES BRUSHING OUR TEETH EVERY DAY, WHY DO WE HAVE TO TAKE A STRING AND "FLOSS" BETWEEN EACH TOOTH.

Mainly because "flossing" is like brushing in the spots where your tooth brush can't reach.... like between your teeth. It's just as important to floss as it is to brush your teeth.

CHICKEN POX - Something that almost every child and some adults will get at some point in their lives is Chicken Pox. Chicken Pox are blisters that form on your skin almost

everywhere on your body (in your hair, around your ears, on your legs and arms, etc.) and are very itchy. Once you've had Chicken Pox, you should never get it again. **But don't scratch.** Scratching could lead to infections and could possibly leave a scar (a mark) that will stay on your skin. There are special lotions that will help make the Chicken Pox less itchy. Chicken Pox takes about 10 days to reach their peak and another 10 - 20 days to fully go away.

CHOKING - When you are choking, something is stuck inside your throat and you can't breathe properly. It could be food that just got stuck on the way down. Someone may have to squeeze your tummy to get whatever is stuck, out. You should never play or run around with small objects in your

mouth like coins (pennies, nickels, dimes, quarters) or small toys as it is very easy to accidentally swallow them and they could get caught half way down your throat. It is also important to chew your food well, or cut up your food into small pieces (especially hot dog weiners) so that big lumps of food do not travel down into your stomach.

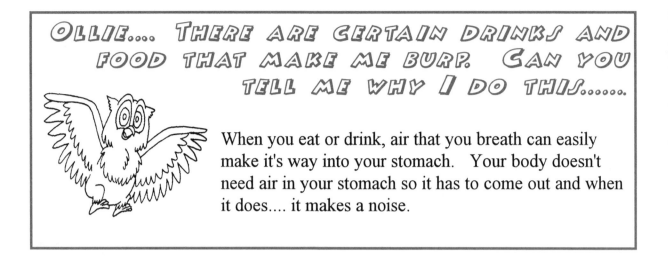

OLLIE.... THERE ARE CERTAIN DRINKS AND FOOD THAT MAKE ME BURP. CAN YOU TELL ME WHY I DO THIS........

When you eat or drink, air that you breath can easily make it's way into your stomach. Your body doesn't need air in your stomach so it has to come out and when it does.... it makes a noise.

COLD SORES - A cold sore usually comes on your lips and looks a bit like a hard blister. There is a special cream that can be put on the cold sore and it usually takes a few days to get better.

COLIC - When a baby has colic, they will cry and cry very loudly for a long time and their face will probably be all red from crying so hard. This is a condition that occurs in babies like your new little brother or sister and it's difficult to know what is causing the baby to cry. Your baby brother or sister

can't tell you or your mom or dad what's wrong but sometimes it's because their little tummy hurts. There is not too much you can do for a baby with colic but your mom or dad may try rocking the baby in a rocking chair or go for a car ride.

COMMON COLD - A cold is a common illness that happens to all of us. With a cold you can have a cough and a sore runny nose. It can make you feel so tired that you really don't feel like doing anything. You should never be scared about getting a common cold. We all get colds at one time or another and we usually get them from other people (from germs that float in the air that you can't see) or sometimes from yucky weather. You should take plenty of liquids like fruit juices, milk and water, get plenty of rest and take some drug store bought medicines and cough syrup that your mom or dad will get for you. This is a good time to do some reading or to watch a bit of TV while you're getting better.

CONCUSSION - A concussion can happen when someone or something hits your head too hard. What happens is the brain tissue inside becomes bruised and there may be some bleeding that might happen inside the head. Your symptoms might include being unconscious (it's like going to sleep for awhile), vomiting, loss of memory and not being able to walk. Like the bruise on your leg or arm, the bruise on your brain will go away in time. Anytime that you receive a serious concussion, someone should take you immediately to a hospital for treatment.

OLLIE.....THE OTHER DAY MY FRIEND BILLY CAME TO SCHOOL AND ALL HIS HAIR WAS GONE. HE SAID THAT HE HAD SOMETHING CALLED CANCER. WHAT IS CANCER?

Cancer is a disease that comes in many forms. It can make people, including some boys and girls, very sick. It is not contagious and there are many cures and treatments for cancer and one of them is chemotherapy. The chemotherapy treatment, which is done in a hospital is what caused Billys hair to fall out. But don't worry as his hair will eventually grow back.

CONSTIPATION - Sometimes when we go to the bathroom to try to have a "bowel movement", there are times when the body will not allow the waste to come out.

Once our bodies take all of the nutrients & energy out of the food we eat, there are leftover parts of the food that our bodies don't need. Our bodies get rid of these in liquid (urine) or in matter (stools or excrement) form. We have to remove these materials from our bodies so that we have room to put more food in to keep our bodies healthy and full of energy. You might have to eat more fruits and vegetables, drink lots of water and take medicines to help your body get rid of the waste.

CROUP - A condition where the voice box (the part of your body that your voice comes from) in your throat is inflamed. This is usually caused by an infection. You will notice this most often when you get up in the morning. Breathing will be harder, your throat will be dry and tight and you'll have a barking type cough. What your parents might do for this is put you back in your bedroom and turn on the humidifier or vaporizer which puts moisture from water into the air to help make your throat feel better.

HEY KIDS, EVER HAVE CHAPPED LIPS? THAT'S WHEN YOUR LIPS GET DRY AND THE SKIN LOSES IT'S MOISTURE AND BECOMES HARD AND CRACKED. THIS CAN HAPPEN ESPECIALLY IN THE WINTER. PROTECT YOURSELF BY BUYING SOME LIP LOTION THAT WILL PLACE MOISTURE BACK INTO THE SKIN OF YOUR LIP AND MAKE IT FEEL BETTER.

CUTS - When you get a cut this is usually from something sharp like broken glass, a knife or even a piece of paper. In most cases cuts get better by themselves. But when a cut is too big to heal properly on its own, a doctor may need to stitch (sew) your skin back together. When it starts to heal it will become itchy; don't scratch it or you will slow the healing process.

CYSTIC FIBROSIS - Is a rare disease that some people are born with which is inherited from their parents. This disease affects the breathing system and the digestive system. Medications and special exercises will be needed to keep healthy.

OLLIE.... WHY DOES MY BACK HURT SOMETIMES WHEN I PLAY?

There are many muscles all over your body and a good number of them are in your back. The muscles help you jump, turn, twist, bend over, bend backwards and the more you exercise, the stronger they will get. When you over do it by lifting something that is too heavy or when you stretch farther than your body is meant to, then your muscles may become sore. Before you start doing a physically demanding activity, you should always warm up the muscles that you are working by stretching them.

DIABETES - occurs in the body when one of the body parts called the pancreas fails to release a substance called insulin. Insulin helps the body turn your food into energy so that you can run & play. What you might have is an increased thirst, feel tired or dizzy, nauseated along with vomiting and a need to use the bathroom more.

You might have to go on a special diet and take medicines so that you can play sports (like baseball, football and hockey) and run & play like all of the other kids.

All living things in our world have a beginning and an end. Flowers bloom in the spring and die in the fall. Insects are born and live a very short time before they die. Animals like cats and dogs live up to 15 years, and people too have a

beginning and an end. People generally live to be somewhere between 80 & 100 years old. People die when there bodies stop working, which happens when they are really old, or from an accident or if they have a disease that can't be cured with treatment yet. If someone special to you has died, such as a grandma or grandpa, you may feel sad for a while. Even though they are not here anymore they will always be with you in your heart.

DIARRHEA - Is when you have to do watery poops in a rush and you keep having to go, and you sometimes can't stop needing to go. This may be because you have eaten something that has upset your tummy and made you ill. Usually this goes away if you don't eat anything for a while and only have clear fluids to drink, so you don't get dehydrated. You can get some medicine to stop the diarrhea and also some cream if your bum is really sore.

OLLIE...WHAT IS BEING DEAF?

DEAFNESS This is when someone can't hear anything with their ears or they can only hear a little bit. It may only happen in one ear, the other ear or even both at the same time.

If you have ever seen someone "talking" with their hands (this is called sign language) this was probably a deaf person or someone "talking" to a deaf person. If you feel that you have a problem hearing your teacher or your parents when they talk, make sure you let both of them know so that they can have it checked out by an ear doctor.

DISLOCATION - Occurs when a bone and its partner bone are not correctly aligned. This is like a toy train that goes off the track, you have to put it back on track in the right line. That is what happens with bones, sometimes they get dislocated, and a doctor will need to put them back in place. If it is not properly aligned when it is put back, it could be made worse which is why a doctor should be seen. It will hurt until it is put back in place.

DIZZINESS - You might have something called dizziness if you are standing still yet you are feeling like you're going

round and round in circles. You might remember, when you have been playing with your friends, spinning around on one spot and when you suddenly stand still - you can hardly keep your balance. When you feel dizzy, you may also feel like vomiting. Try lying down for awhile to help the dizziness go away and make sure to raise your feet a few inches above your head.

OLLIE.... WHY ARE MY EARS SO IMPORTANT?

Hearing is one of the five senses (the others are taste, touch, smell and sight). Ears allow us to hear the sounds that everything makes. From the horn on a car to a chirping of a baby chick. Never stick any objects in your ears as it could cause severe damage to your hearing.

EARACHES - There are times when our ears all of a sudden start aching. It could be because you have a cold or that you have an infection in the ear. If your ears hurt on the inside, your parents will help by putting ear ache medicine in it or using a warm hot water bottle to make it feel better.   If it is an ear infection, then a doctor would suggest some antibiotics to help take the infection away. Objects smaller than your little finger (of any kind) should never be placed in your ears as they could harm them.

ECZEMA - This is a rash on the skin which is itchy and dry feeling. Sometimes when it is scratched a clear watery liquid comes out. Usually this is worse in the winter when our homes are dry. A cream is put on the eczema to help clear it up. The best things to do are to wash or shower regularly and don't scratch it.

FAINTING - When you faint, in simple words, it's like suddenly going to sleep when you're not tired. It's due to a brief loss of blood in the brain and can happen if there is emotional stress in your life, low sugar levels in the blood, or just by being physically tired. The person who fainted should wake up again after several seconds or a few minutes and should remain in a sitting or lying down position for a least ten minutes until their body has had a chance to return to normal.

FEVER - Your body has a temperature inside of you set at 98.6 Fahrenheit / 37 degrees Celsius. When your body has a fever, the body temperature increases so that it can better fight the germs and diseases in your body. There are a number of medicines to help relieve the pain and to return the body back to normal temperature. You might have to have a cool cloth to put on your forehead.

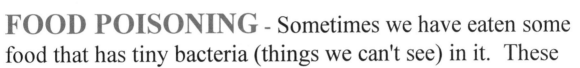

OLLIE..... WHEN I EAT MY BURGER AND FRIES, WHERE DO THEY GO?

Many children ask me this. The food that you eat everyday is extremely important in giving your body energy to do everyday things like running, jumping and playing. After you chew up your food in your mouth, it travels down into your stomach. Your stomach is where food goes and where your body will remove all of the energy from the food.

FOOD POISONING - Sometimes we have eaten some food that has tiny bacteria (things we can't see) in it. These bacteria will not be in food when it is cooked properly either at home or when we go out to a restaurant. However there are times when food (mostly meat) is not cooked as fully as it should and when we eat the food, it makes us sick. What happens is that you could throw up (called vomiting) all the food which you just ate or you may have diarrhea (see Diarrhea page 28) and stomach cramps anywhere from one to five hours after eating.

Sometimes a fever comes with it and it may stay for anywhere from 12 to 24 hours until the food leaves the body. For more serious cases of food poisoning, you will go to the doctor's office or a hospital.

EYES - Sight is one of the five senses and is one of the most important. Without our eyes we could not see where we are going and the many wonders of the world. Some people have to wear glasses to see better as their eyesight may not be as strong as it should be. Eyes should be protected in playing any sport where there is a chance of them getting injured (eg. playing hockey, racquetball, football, etc.) or at some jobs (welders, painters, carpenters, etc.). If you are

reading a book, looking at pictures or watching TV and they don't look clear to you, then you may require glasses. A check-up with an optometrist would be in order. If you get something in your eyes that hurts, don't rub them but call out for help. Rubbing them could make it worse. People sometimes have allergic reactions that are caused by a wide variety of things and make your eyes sore, itchy and all red. There are medicines that you can buy at the pharmacy that will help make them feel better.

FRACTURES - There are hundreds of bones in your body. When you fall or bang into something really hard you may fracture a bone. If this happens, you cannot tell, so you will have to go and get a picture taken by a special camera (x-ray) that sees inside your body. Stay very still so the doctor can get good pictures. This special picture will tell the doctor if the bone is fractured or not. If it is fractured, don't worry because bones can heal themselves if they are placed in a cast. You might have to wear this for several weeks and go to sleep with it on.

FROSTBITE - Frostbite occurs when skin has been over-exposed to the cold so that the tissues (not Kleenex, but tiny cells that make up your skin) have been frozen. Frostbitten skin will feel numb and will turn red and will be painful as it warms up. Serious frostbite needs to be treated right away by a doctor. You can treat frostbite yourself by first getting out of the cold, then gently warming the frostbitten area by putting it in contact with warm skin.... do not rub. Do not use a heating pad and never stick the frostbitten area in hot water.

KIDS...IT'S VERY IMPORTANT TO START GOOD GROOMING HABITS WHEN YOU ARE YOUNG BECAUSE THIS IS NOT AS EASY WHEN YOU GET OLDER. REGULAR SHOWERS OR BATHS EVERY DAY ARE IMPORTANT TO ME SO THAT I CAN GET ALL THE DUST AND DIRT OFF AND FEEL REALLY CLEAN.....AND SO CAN YOU.

HAY FEVER - You may recall that we talked about allergies earlier on in this book. Allergies are something that we have a reaction to when we shouldn't. Well hay fever is when we are allergic to something at a certain time of the year like summer when there is a lot of pollen from flowers, grass and weeds in the air. You may find yourself sneezing & sniffling, your nose is plugged and you may have earaches and a fever. If these things affect you, avoid areas that make you worse. Your doctor will know what is the best medicine to take.

HEADACHES - Almost everyone will have a headache at some time or another. Your head will feel like it's being squeezed, your eyes like they're being pinched. Most headaches will go away after a few hours, either by themselves, or by resting, or by taking some medicine for headaches.

HEAT RASH - A heat rash can happen when your body gets too hot. It starts to sweat and the sweat dries too quickly. Your skin will get sore and itchy. A doctor may give you some cream to put on. Sometimes babies get heat rashes when they have been bundled up for too long in a hot place and their skin can't breathe properly. Often just allowing a baby to play a bit without a diaper on will help to clear up the heat rash.

HEAT STROKE (OR SUN STROKE) -

This is a condition when a person's body has been exposed to too much heat for too long. The body is unable to put back the water lost by perspiring and the body temperature suddenly rises. This problem usually happens to athletes or people who do very hard work in hot weather. You might have to move into a cool area and have fruit juice or water to cool yourself down, or you may have to rub ice on your body or soak in a cool bath.

HYPERVENTILATION - The air that you breathe contains oxygen, which you need in order to live. If you start breathing too fast, your body won't be getting enough oxygen. You may feel like you are suffocating, and you will feel tingly and faint. By relaxing and taking deep slow breaths, your breathing should return to normal.

OLLIE....WHEN I'M PLAYING GAMES WITH MY FRIENDS LIKE SKIPPING AND HOP SCOTCH, THE HEELS ON THE BOTTOM OF MY FEET HURT. WHY?

That's a good one. At one time or another, all children will experience soreness in their heels - which are at the bottom/back of your feet. It is usually from jumping or running on hard surfaces. One way to help this soreness is to place thick heel pads inside your shoes to make it softer on your heels while the soreness has a chance to go away.

INFLUENZA - Having the flu, as influenza is most often called, means that you have picked up a viral infection that will more often give you a fever, the chills, a cough, you'll feel tired and your muscles will be sore. It is a contagious infection, which means that others can

get it if they are near you. Almost everyone gets the flu at one time or another in their lives and there are many medicines to help you feel better. You might have the flu anywhere from 3 to 10 days before you get better.

INGROWN TOENAILS -
This is something that happens when a toenail grows quickly and actually curves and grows into your skin. If this happens it will get really sore and you will have to go to the doctor.

WHY DO MY FRIENDS SAY THAT I LOOK LIKE MY PARENTS?

When the same characteristics like colour of eyes, colour of hair, same looks, same height, etc., are passed down from parents to their children.... we call this heredity. There are 46 chromosomes in every cell of the human body. When a baby is born, 23 chromosomes comes from each parent to equal 46. That's why you look like your mom and dad.

LARYNGITIS - Our voice
box, or larynx, is what allows us to
speak. If the larynx becomes
inflamed or irritated, either because
of a virus or an infection, this is
called laryngitis. The throat will
feel raw and tickley, the voice will
become scratchy.

LEUKEMIA - Is a form of cancer
in the blood which affects the white
blood cells. White blood cells fight
infections. You can't see that the blood
has white cells because of all the
bright red cells. If you have leukemia
your doctor will have to try to get your
blood mixing properly. Doctors have
all kinds of things they can do to help
your blood. They may give you
medicine or use another kind of
treatment to help you get better.

OLLIE..... WHAT ARE HICCUPS?

Everybody gets hiccups!!! Hiccups are not harmful
and they normally last for only a few minutes.
Hiccups happens when air is stuck in your voice box
and makes a funny noise when it comes out.

MEASLES - Is a skin disease where you get lots of little red spots all over your body. You may also get a temperature. Measles do not last very long, and you will have to stay home so that you don't give it to your friends. When the spots are getting better they will itch so try not to scratch them.

MONONUCLEOSIS (MONO) - A disease where you just feel tired and don't know what is wrong. It is a virus which takes a long time to go away. Only through a lab test can you be sure you have Mono. If you have Mono the doctor will say you should get plenty of rest and drink lots of fluids.

MUMPS - A disease that causes painful swellings just below and in front of your ears, it makes you look a bit like a chipmunk with a mouthful of nuts. Mumps takes several days to go away and the doctor can give you some medicine to help you feel better.

OLLIE.....SOMETIMES IN THE MORNING, I WAKE UP AND MY VOICE SOUNDS DIFFERENT AND MY THROAT IS SO SORE. WHY IS THIS?

HOARSENESS - This has nothing to do with real horses. This is when your voice sounds different as a result of screaming or from an allergy, the croup or something called laryngitis. Sometimes, because of it, you can hardly talk because it affects your vocal cords (the area in your throat that allows you to speak). If this happens to you, rest your throat by speaking very quietly or not at all for awhile; drink warm liquids and breathe some steam from a vaporizer (your mom and dad will show you what that is). It should clear up in a day or two.

MUSCULAR DYSTROPHY - In your body there are things called muscles which control all of your body's movement. When you have muscular dystrophy, your muscles get weak and you may feel clumsy. They get so weak sometimes that you will have to wear braces or use a wheelchair. There are a lot of treatments available including physical therapies that can help.

42

NEPHRITIS - Is when your kidneys (which filter all the body fluids to make them clean) get inflamed and are not able to do what they are supposed to do. You need to get them working again as soon as possible. You will see a doctor to have some special tests done to find out why things aren't working properly. Medicine may be given to you or you may have to have dialysis. This is a special way to help your body clean your blood.

NOSE BLEED - When blood comes out of your nose. This is another common occurrence which can happen when you are young or even when you are a grown-up. It can be caused from someone bumping your nose while playing or when your nose is dry or even when you pick your nose. To stop the nose bleed.....you or your parents should pinch your nostrils together for about 5 or 10 minutes (sometimes you may have to do this a couple of times) or place something cold (a cold cloth with ice) against the back of the neck or the forehead or the upper lip. This constricts the blood vessels to stop the bleeding.

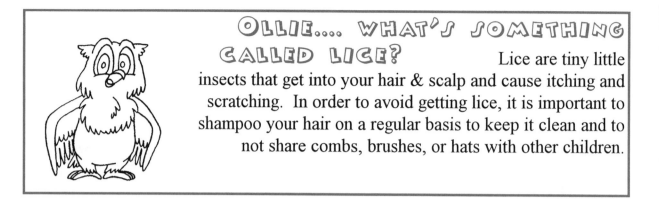

Lice are tiny little insects that get into your hair & scalp and cause itching and scratching. In order to avoid getting lice, it is important to shampoo your hair on a regular basis to keep it clean and to not share combs, brushes, or hats with other children.

PNEUMONIA - A disease of your lungs which are like paper bags/balloons inside your chest. Your lungs fill up with air when you breathe in and empty when you breathe out. Sometimes fluids get inside and these fluids need to be removed. A doctor can give you special medication to help get rid of these fluids, so you can breath much easier. You may have to visit a hospital or stay at home with a vaporizers and take medication to cure it.

Poison Ivy is a plant that grows outdoors and will give you a rash if you touch it. The rash can be quite small or fairly large depending on how much of the plant touches your skin. If you try to rub it off or touch it and then touch another part of your body, you will spread the rash. You can protect yourself when you are in the forest, in the bushes or in dense brush by wearing long socks and pants so that your skin is not showing. There may be a medicine to fix the rash at the drug store or you may have to see the doctor.

OLLIE...WHAT ARE OUR LUNGS FOR?

In your body where your chest is, you have two lungs that are like wet balloons. When you breathe in air, your lungs fill up and get larger like when you blow up a balloon. When you push all of the air out of your body, your chest gets a bit smaller because you've pushed all the air out. You breath in air and breath out air without even thinking about it.... your body just knows to breathe in a certain amount to supply all of your body cells.

POISONING - **When children consume poisons, they have taken a substance that could seriously harm and damage their bodies.** All young children are very curious and even though they may have been taught and instructed lots of times by their mom and dad not to, they can still make mistakes by touching or drinking poisons. There are many things around your house that are poisonous. Ask your mom & dad to show you the ones in your house so that you know what not to touch. If there is an accident and you take a poison, then your parents will immediately read the warning label on the poison container for instructions on what to do. If there isn't any, they will immediately call the poison control centre in your community for instructions. The phone number should be posted near the phone (and in the back of this book) along with the police department, fire department, your doctor and other emergency services.

PUNCTURE WOUNDS -

Something that happens to kids when having an object like a stick, knife, pin or nail stick into your foot, hand, or leg. A puncture wound to the chest, neck and head, as well as other parts of the body can be very serious and a doctor must be seen immediately.   He might take an

x-ray to see if there is anything in the wound and may stitch it up or place a band-aid over it. A tetanus shot may be required to help the wound to heal.

RASHES - These are caused by all kinds of things such as measles, chicken pox, poison ivy, allergies, heat or any of a long list of various illnesses. Many rashes go away quickly. Most are itchy as they are healing and they get better quicker if you don't scratch them. If the rash continues for several days and your Mom and Dad don't know what it is then you will go to see the doctor.

OLLIE....WHEN I WAS IN THE HOSPITAL VISITING A FRIEND, THERE WAS SOMETHING CALLED AN INTER......AN INTRAVE......IN HER ARM. WHAT IS IT?

You mean an Intravenous. An IV, as it's often called, is a device that feeds medicines or fluids directly into a patients veins. A person's body is able to absorb the fluids and medicines much faster from an IV than by taking them into the mouth. The IV is a clear plastic bag hung on a pole containing fluid or medicine. Plastic tubes connect the bag to a needle that is placed into a vein (in the wrist or hand) so that the fluid or medicine goes directly into the blood stream.

SCABIES - Is a skin infection that occurs when a tiny almost invisible insect (called a mite) burrows into your skin. Your skin will feel very itchy, especially at night, and you will have thin squiggly lines on your skin that look like they were drawn by a pencil. Your doctor will give you a special cream to get rid of the mites & stop the itching.

SHOCK - If you are in shock, something big has happened to you and you don't really understand what and why. It could have happened in an accident where you had a big cut and lost a lot of blood. You will have to see a doctor immediately if you are suffering from shock. You may feel cold when it is hot; you may feel hot, when it is cold or you may be disoriented (confused) and not know who or where you are.

OLLIE....WHEN I GO TO THE DOCTORS OFFICE, HE GIVES ME NEEDLES WITH VACCINE IN IT..... HOW COME?

IMMUNIZATIONS - Yes, this is a big word for some young children and if you say it in parts .... it's easier - IM MU NI ZA TIONS. This is placing very special vaccine into your body to prevent serious diseases. Years ago diseases like (these may be tough words to say) Diphtheria, Tetanus, Whooping Cough, Polio, Measles, Mumps etc., made children very very sick which no longer needs to happen. Most immunizations are given to you by needle when you are quite young (birth to around 15 months old) and you probably don't remember getting them. You will get one more needle usually just before you enter school and it may hurt a little bit (like a mosquito bite or when your brother or sister pinches you). The vaccine in the needle is very important in helping to keep you healthy and strong as you continue to grow.

SORE THROAT / STREP THROAT- Germs that cause colds also cause sore throats and have often the same affect as the common cold. The treatment is usually the same as for a cold but if you have a throat that is really sore you will see a doctor. It may be tonsillitis, a sore and red swollen part at the back of your mouth. You can sometimes see how red it is in

48

the mirror. It may also have little white spots. The doctor may take a swab, using a cotton ball on a stick. The doctor will have to tickle the back of your throat to get a good swab. Then the swab is sent away for some tests to be done on it to find out if it is what is called a **strep** throat. This is a bad sore throat and you will have to have some medicine.

SPRAINS - Joints are all the places in our bodies where two bones are joined together: fingers, wrists, hips, elbows, ankles. Joints are surrounded and protected by stretchy tissues called ligaments. When the ligaments get torn and the joint gets twisted out of place, we call it a sprain. It will feel sore and tender and will look bruised and swollen. You may have to wear a sling.

OLLIE....WHY AM I SCARED SOMETIMES WHEN I GO TO BED?

NIGHT FEARS - When you go to bed, your bedroom can sometimes be a lonely place when the only person in it is you. You shouldn't be scared to go to bed because your mom or dad are near by and will be there if you need them.

Our brains sometimes plays tricks on us by making you think that you hear a noise, or see something that really isn't there. To make you feel better try a night light which will stay on all night and you can see everything in your room - if you happen to wake up.

49

STOMACH ACHE (TUMMY ACHE) -The

stomach is where all of the food is changed into energy. When you have a stomach ache, you have sharp pains or your stomach may feel like it's upside down. You can get a tummy ache from eating too much candy or it could be because you haven't eaten and are hungry or have the flu. You might have to lie down for awhile or take some medicine to feel better.

STREP INFECTIONS - Most commonly affect the

throat which is where you swallow your food and liquids. There are all kinds of strep infections which are quite serious. The most common one is strep throat (see sore throat), which is very sore and highly contagious. This means that anyone who comes near you is likely to catch it, too. Some strep infections are mouth infections and some are skin infections.

NIGHTMARES - While you are sleeping, you may have something called a dream. A dream is when your brain is still working, showing you pictures and stories and even words. We all have dreams and most of the time they are happy pleasant dreams. But sometimes we have scary dreams called nightmares, that are usually caused by anxieties and fears that we have had while we were awake. You may wake up after a scary dream frightened, crying, or even screaming. Your mom or dad will help you calm down after a nightmare by holding and hugging you and talking to you in soft tones. After a short time, you will then be able to go back to sleep.

STYES - When part of the eyelid gets infected and swells up this is often known as a sty. There are special ointments and eye drops to help get rid of styes. If you get them often or over again it could be caused by something in your diet or you may just be very tired and not feeling well. The doctor can find out what is causing them.

SUNBURN - A sunburn is just that....a burn that the sun gave you. On a bright clear summer day, there is a chance that if you are out in the sun too long, the sun's rays could burn your skin. The best thing

51

that you could do for a sun burn is not to get one in the first place. All you have to do is make sure that you are properly covered with light clothes and a hat and stay in shaded areas for part of the day. Also, if your skin is exposed use lots and lots of suntan lotion. Use suntan lotions with 30 SPF or higher. If a sunburn does occur, it could range from being just a little bit sore (a little redness may show up) or a serious burn where the skin could become very painful and blisters could form. After a more serious sunburn, your skin will become dry and flaky and sometimes the skin will peal off, but do not worry..... your body has made a new fresh layer of skin underneath to keep you protected. Your doctor has special medicine to help relieve the pain of your burn.

OLLIE - KIDS, DO YOU PERSPIRE SOMETIMES.... I SURE DO. WHEN I'M FLYING AROUND IN THE HOT SUN, THE WATER IN MY BODY COMES THROUGH MY SKIN AND FORMS LITTLE WATER DROPLETS CALLED SWEAT OR PERSPIRATION. YOU HAVE PROBABLY HAD THIS HAPPEN TO YOU WHEN YOU PLAY WITH YOUR FRIENDS OR WHEN YOU EXERCISE AT SCHOOL. IT'S A VERY NATURAL THING TO HAPPEN AS YOUR BODY IS TRYING TO COOL ITSELF OFF BY PERSPIRING.

SWALLOWED OBJECTS

- Swallowing objects like small coins, plastic toys or other small items can be scary. The best thing for children is to never place items in their mouths, even if they are just fooling around because accidents do happen. Almost all of these small size objects will go into the child's stomach and will pass right out of the body - however, they could get caught in the throat. The doctor may take an X-ray of your throat and neck area to see exactly where the object is stuck. Then he will take a special instrument, reach down in your throat and take out the object. If you have a baby brother or sister, then you should help your mom and dad by making sure there are no coins (money) or small objects within reach that the baby can place in his or her mouth and choke on.

TEETHING - By the time that you are able to read this or even by the time that your parents will be reading this to you, your mouth will have a full set of teeth. When you are born, however, you have no teeth at all and it is in your first 2 -3 years that all of your teeth grow in. Usually at 3 - 6 months old, your first 4 teeth will start to show. You don't remember it now but

teething was a bit painful because they had to grow out through your gums in your mouth. When you are around 6-7 years old, your "baby" teeth will start to fall out because your "grown-up" teeth are beginning to form underneath and they are pushing your baby teeth out. You will see that your grown up teeth are quite a bit bigger than your baby teeth.

TONSILLITIS - Tonsils are at the back of the mouth and are used to filter out harmful germs. Sometimes when they have too many germs to filter they become sore. You will have trouble swallowing and may feel like you have the flu. You will have to get plenty of rest and drink lots of soothing fluids, and sometimes you will have to go to the doctor for him to check your throat and give you some medicine.

TOOTHACHE - Can be caused when you have a cavity. Your tooth feels sore to touch, and ice cream or a hot drink touching your tooth can make you jump. You might have

fallen and chipped off a piece of your tooth. If this is what is happening, you will have to visit the dentist to fix it. Inside your teeth there are things called nerves and when these get opened up they are very sore. The dentist will cover them again with a filling.

OLLIE - MY MOM AND DAD KEEP TELLING ME TO SIT UP STRAIGHT FOR GOOD POSTURE. WHAT DOES THIS MEAN?

Your parents are right, you must always continue to sit up and stand up straight in order for your body to be straight and strong when you get older. As you are growing, the part of your body called the spine is growing with you - which is the bone that runs down the middle of your back. As the spine grows, it is very helpful to have good posture to help support all of the other body parts so that your whole body can be strong.

VIRAL INFECTIONS (A VIRUS)

A virus is bad germs that get into the body and make you feel sick. With a combination of time and medicines, most virus's will eventually leave your body, returning you to your normal healthy self.

KIDS....DO YOU KNOW WHY YOU HAVE TO SLEEP? WELL OUR BODY REQUIRES A CERTAIN AMOUNT OF REST EACH DAY SO THAT IT CAN FUNCTION AT IT'S BEST. APPROX. 1/3 OF OUR LIFE IS SPENT SLEEPING AND FOR YOUNG PEOPLE, 8 - 10 HOURS OF SLEEP A DAY IS IMPORTANT SO YOU CAN GROW UP TO BE BIG AND STRONG.

VISION PROBLEMS - The eyes are what we use to see the world. Sometimes they don't work properly and we have to wear glasses to help them. Some children have to wear them all the time some just wear them to see up close & some

just to see farther away. Some children have to wear a patch on their eye for a while to help their "lazy eye" get stronger.

EIOUF

FOEPRY

GFYER

VOMITING - Throwing up. Vomiting is when you put food or liquids into your stomach and your stomach rebels and sends it back out of your mouth (yuk). Children vomit right from the time they are babies but never get used to it. It still is an uncomfortable thing for anyone to have happen but not to worry as it is quite common. Sometimes vomiting can be caused by certain foods or drinks or quite often, the result of a cold or the flu.

KIDS..THERE MAY BE TIMES THAT YOUR BODY IS NOT GETTING ENOUGH NUTRITIONAL FOODS. VITAMINS AND MINERALS CAN HELP ENSURE THAT YOU ARE GETTING A DAILY BALANCE OF NUTRIENTS FOR YOUR BODY.

WARTS - Warts are small little bumps that appear on our skin and are harmless. Warts are caused by a virus and they can be spread by contact with the wart or by scratching it. Warts can stay on your body for a number of years and then will suddenly disappear. There are medicines at the drug store that may be used to try and get rid of them.

OLLIE..... I'VE SEEN TEENAGERS DO SOMETHING CALLED SMOKING. WHY DO THEY DO IT AND CAN IT HURT YOU?

Most teenagers who smoke cigarettes do it to show off to their friends. They think it is a cool thing to do and yes it can hurt you. It's very bad for you and can lead to serious illnesses once you get older. My best advice to you is never start smoking at all during your lifetime and you'll be wise like me.

WHOOPING COUGH - This is a really bad cough that has a funny sound as well as the normal type of cough. It doesn't happen too often these days but it keeps you awake for long periods and you might have to go to the doctor to get some medicine to help.

SPEECH / STUTTERING - We talk with each other through speech (sounds made with our mouths and vocal chords). Some people have trouble talking for a number of reasons such as physical or emotional problems. Missing teeth, a different shaped nose or tongue and even problems with the lungs or larynx (our voice box) may interfere with normal sounds and speech.

When a person stutters, it is when they repeat a sound of a word several times before you hear the whole word. An example of this is when a word such as Car is tried, it might come out like CaCaCaCa Car or Bike sound like BBBBBike. Good results in correcting stuttering have been made with the help of speech therapy either in class or individual sessions.

OLLIE.... THERE ARE TIMES WHEN I TAKE DEEP BREATHS OF AIR THAT MY FRIENDS CALL YAWNING. WHAT IS HAPPENING WHEN I YAWN.

You know what kids.... I yawn too!! It's usually because the body needs more air so it can work better. We breath in and out all the time, which is automatic but sometimes the body needs just a little bit more so we yawn.

OUR GRANDMAS AND GRANDPAS

There are special people in our lives who we call our Grandparents. They are your Mom & Dad's... Mom and Dad! Other names people have for grandparents are Granny & Papa, Gran & Gramps, Nanny and Papa and a host of other names. They are quite a bit older than you are and have many wise and interesting stories to tell. We should all respect our grandparents as they've been around for many years and you wouldn't be here if it weren't for them.

You may notice that as they get older, a number of changes that may occur in their lives. Besides retiring (not having to go to a job every day) & collecting a pension, they will have time to travel, or work on hobbies or just take it easy. Your grandparents are also more likely to develop aging ailments. These ailments may include conditions called Arthritis (page 16); High Blood Pressure;

Alzheimer's (page 14); some loss of hair / hair turning grey in colour; Vision problems (needing glasses); and their movements becoming slower.

They may have to make more frequent trips to the doctor to receive proper medication and treatment. The advances in medicines and the knowledge of how to properly treat people have been tremendous during the last number of years and many more breakthroughs are sure to happen in the years to come.

After working for most of their lives, our Grandmas and Grandpa's deserve a chance to relax and take it easy, to go on vacations & holidays and to explore various parts of what our country and our world has to offer.

If you get a chance in the near future, offer your help to your Grandma or Grandpa do the dishes, take out the trash, rake leaves or shovel their sidewalk for them in the winter.... they'll appreciate it!!!

WELL KIDS, IT'S BEEN A HOOT SHARING ALL OF MY HEALTH TIPS WITH YOU IN THIS BOOK. I HOPE THAT I HAVE GIVEN YOU LOTS OF GOOD INFORMATION ABOUT THINGS YOU WANTED TO KNOW.

I'VE LEFT AN AREA IN THE BACK OF THE BOOK FOR YOU AND YOUR MOM AND DAD TO WRITE DOWN EMERGENCY PHONE NUMBERS AND TO KEEP A RECORD OF ALL YOUR SHOTS.

REMEMBER, YOU NEED TO GET PLENTY OF REST, EXERCISE AND A PROPER DIET TO GROW UP TO KEEP HEALTHY AND TO BE BIG, STRONG AND WISE LIKE ME.

KIDS.....STUDY HARD IN SCHOOL, LISTEN TO YOUR PARENTS AND ALWAYS SAY NO TO DRUGS. BYE FOR NOW!

IMMUNIZATION RECORD

TYPE	CHILD/DATE		REMARKS

IMMUNIZATION RECORD

TYPE	CHILD/DATE		REMARKS

EMERGENCY PHONE NUMBERS

HOSPITAL _____

POLICE _____

FIRE _____

POISON TREATMENT _____

AMBULANCE _____

FAMILY DOCTOR _____

PHARMACY _____

DENTIST _____

_____ _____